Vikings

CONTENTS

© Aladdin Books Ltd

Designed and produced by
Aladdin Books Ltd
70 Old Compton Street
London W1

First published in
Great Britain in 1984 by
Hamish Hamilton Children's Books
Garden House
57-59 Long Acre
London WC2 E9JZ

Printed in Belgium

British Library Cataloguing in Publication Data
Vikings.—(Find out about)
 1. Vikings—Juvenile literature
 I. Series
 948′.02   D265

ISBN 0-241-11275-3

Certain illustrations have previously appeared in the ''Closer Look''
series published by Hamish Hamilton.

FIND OUT ABOUT

Vikings

JILL HUGHES

Illustrated by

IVAN LAPPER

Consultant

JOHN REEVE

Hamish Hamilton · London

Pirates!

More than a thousand years ago, the Vikings sailed from their homes in Norway, Sweden, and Denmark to attack lands to the south. The Vikings had fast wooden ships, and they were good sailors. At first, they sailed over the seas in search of treasure, because their own lands were too rugged and poor to give a good living to all their people.

When the Viking ships appeared, men, women and children ran away in fear. The Vikings were terrifying and cruel. But they were also brave and clever. Although they had no compasses, they sailed their ships as far west as America, and eastwards down the rivers of Russia. The history of several countries was changed by these adventurers from the far north.

The stone carving above comes from Lindisfarne, off the north of England. It shows the Viking raiders armed with swords and axes.

The Vikings robbed homes and churches. They took coins and precious glass, as well as richly decorated gold and silver treasures.

The Viking homelands

The Vikings were called "the Northmen" by the people they terrified. They came from three Scandinavian countries – Norway, Sweden and Denmark. Norway is very rocky. The sea cuts into the land making fjords. Sweden has many lakes and rivers, and huge pine forests. Denmark is a flat land with rich green fields.

Many of the Vikings who lived along the Scandinavian sea coasts knew how to build boats and sail them. The languages of these lands were very similar as well, so someone from Sweden, for example, could understand the speech of someone from Norway. At first, the three countries did not have their own kings. Instead, each one had many chiefs.

Viking farms in Norway lay beside inlets in the coast, called fjords.

The law of the land

Most of the Viking chiefs were brave fighters who could lead their men in battle. With the treasure they captured from countries such as England, they could buy land, horses and cows. The more land a man had, the more important he was.

Chiefs could not do exactly as they liked. There were laws which had to be obeyed. Groups of men formed themselves into councils, to see that people obeyed the law. These councils were called Things. Some of the biggest Things were almost like our parliaments today. If one man killed another man in a fight, the men of the Thing made him pay money to the dead man's family.

A fight to the death.

7

8

House and home

Most Viking houses had just one big room in which everyone lived, including their livestock. It would have been very dark and smoky inside. The fireplace was in the middle of the room, and as there was no chimney, the smoke had to escape through a hole in the roof. There was not much furniture. People slept on benches of earth, or wood, piled up with straw or furs.

A Viking family in their wooden home.

Buildings

There were different kinds of houses. Some were made of wood and looked rather like log cabins. Others had a framework of wood, but the walls were made of thin sticks woven together like basketwork. The holes were filled with mud and straw. Until recently, in the far north of Scotland, there were houses of stone with grass roofs – another way in which the Vikings built their homes.

A stone house with a grass roof in Scotland.

9

Dragon ships

The Vikings built several different kinds of ships. They had sturdy boats for carrying goods from one coastal town to another. They also had great warships. These were called "longships" because of their long, narrow shape. Each longship could carry a whole band of warriors. They could be rowed, but also carried sails. When the wind filled these sails, the long, narrow ships seemed to fly through the water. The front of a ship, called the prow, was sometimes carved with the head of a dragon. It made the ship look like a fierce sea monster.

Viking prows.

Building and carving a Viking longship.

The best ships in the world

Nobody else built ships like the Vikings. None of their neighbours had ships with sails, so none could travel as quickly. Because of the shallow shape of their ships, the Vikings could sail them up shallow rivers, as well as across the deep Atlantic ocean to Iceland, and even to America. In fact, they could even sail their small ships right on to the beach. But the ships were big enough to take men and horses, and all the things they needed to camp on shore. Some of these ships were buried with dead Viking chiefs.

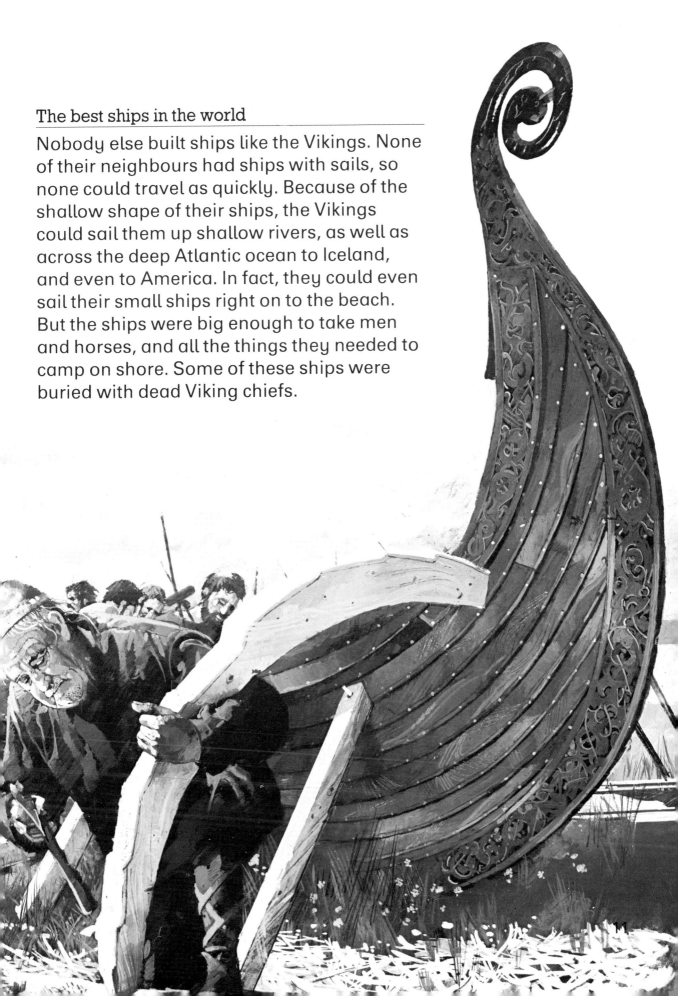

Towns and markets

We have seen what good sailors the Vikings were. At home, in their own lands, they were good farmers too. They grew corn and barley, and kept animals such as cows, horses and pigs. The Vikings were also clever at making things which they exchanged for food, a sword perhaps, or other supplies they needed. They made swords, axes and nails from iron, and beautiful jewellery from gold and silver. But they were best at working in wood. Their longships were made of oak and pine. The Vikings who sailed to other lands sometimes took swords and furs with them. They swapped them for silver or gold, or goods made by the people of these lands. This sort of exchange is called trading.

Markets

Swapping, or trading goods, was usually done at markets. The town of Hedeby, in Denmark, had a very big market. Merchants came from as far away as France, Russia, or even the Arab countries to trade there. They exchanged their goods for furs, amber and walrus ivory.

Coins from many countries were brought to Hedeby.

Craftsmen and merchants on a busy market day in Hedeby.

Wood, metal, and bone

The Vikings used wood, metal and bone to make beautiful and useful things. To the Vikings, their iron swords and spears were not just weapons for fighting. They had a special, almost magical power. The picture shows how a spear was made out of several strips of iron. The iron was heated to make it soft. Then the strips were twisted together and beaten into shape with a hammer. Because several strips of metal were used, the spearhead was very strong. The Viking blacksmiths usually decorated their swords and spears with beautiful patterns. On some they wrote magic spells with letters called runes. Blacksmiths also made more ordinary things, such as padlocks and keys. The lock below was opened by raising the key to bend open the end of the shackle.

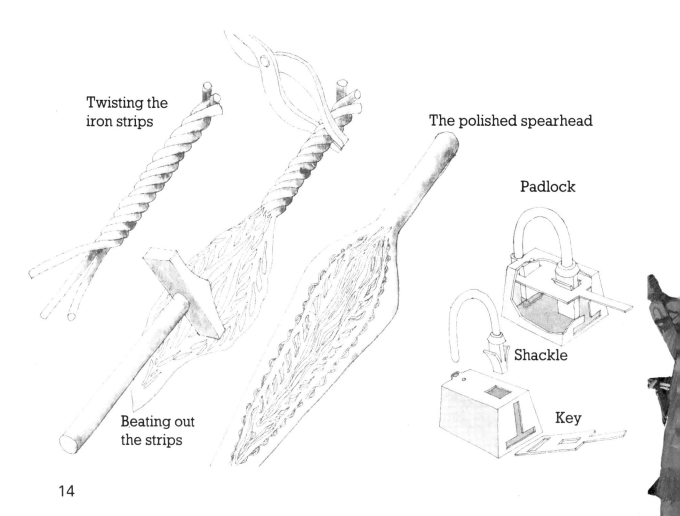

Twisting the iron strips

The polished spearhead

Padlock

Beating out the strips

Shackle

Key

Carpenters and woodcarvers

Many carpenters were needed to build a ship. Some cut down the trees and chopped them into planks. Others smoothed the rough planks and fixed them together. They used iron axes and chisels.

The Vikings did not have much furniture, but other useful things, such as buckets, were made out of wood. Like the blacksmiths with their swords, the carpenters often decorated their work. The carved dragon's head in the picture comes from a ship which was buried with a Viking princess. So were the sledge and the little bed.

This comb is made out of a red deer's antler. The teeth of the comb fit into a little carrying case. Spoons and needles were also made out of bone or antler.

Viking woodwork

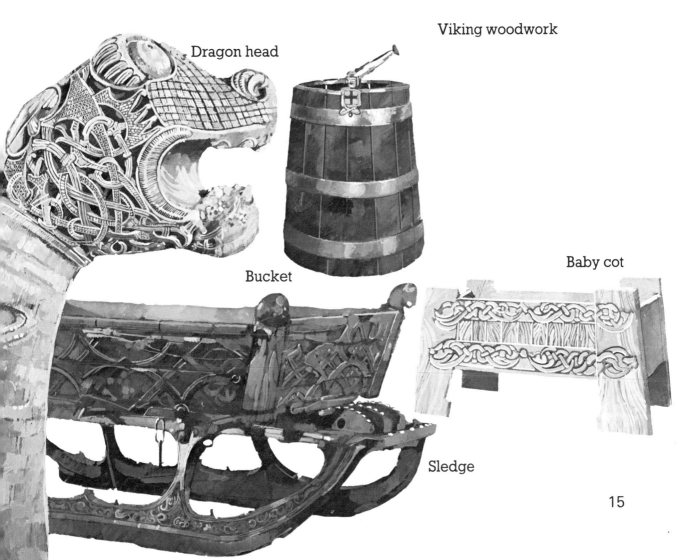

Dragon head

Bucket

Baby cot

Sledge

15

New lands

Once they had learnt what other lands were like, some of the Vikings began to think of leaving their own homes forever, and settling somewhere better. In Norway, a very powerful king ruled, named Harald Fairhair.

Some of the Norwegian lords hated his high-handed ways. They left Norway in search of a country where they could govern themselves. They sailed westwards to Iceland. Here they set up their own "kingdom without a king." Instead, they governed themselves by a law court and parliament called the Althing, which met every summer to pass laws.

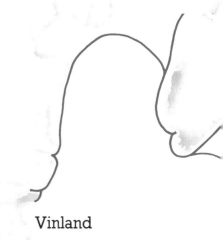

Vinland

The darker colours show the Viking homelands, and areas where they settled.

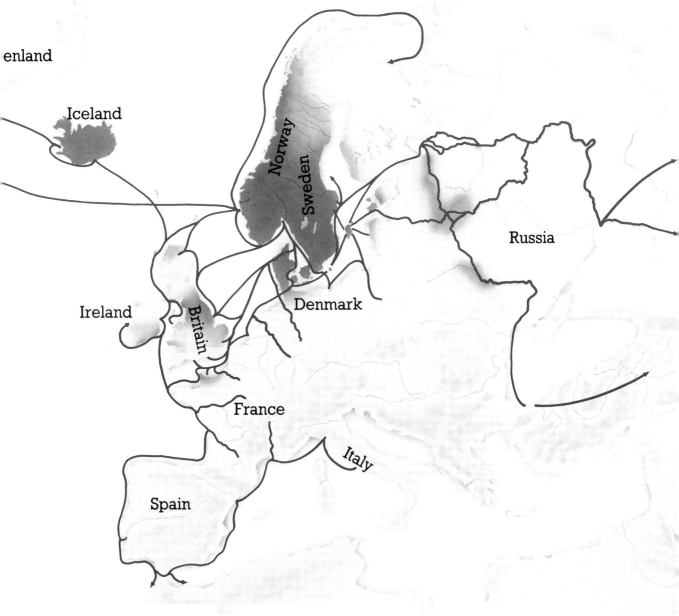

enland

Iceland

Norway

Sweden

Russia

Ireland

Britain

Denmark

France

Italy

Spain

Explorers
The map shows some of the routes taken by the Vikings. Although they sailed to America, Russia, Spain and the Mediterranean, they settled in only a few places (the brown patches on the map) including Britain, Iceland and Russia. Perhaps these countries reminded them of home.

Stories and songs
The Vikings loved to make up stories and poems about battles and the brave men who fought in them. They told stories, too, about their adventures in faraway places. At first these stories were not written down, but memorized and sung on special days at feasts. The stories were called sagas.

Rollo and the King of France
Rollo was the leader of a band of Danish Vikings who attacked the coast of France. At last, the French king, Charles, persuaded Rollo to be his friend. He allowed Rollo to rule over Normandy in France. So Rollo agreed to fight for the king against any other Vikings!

The Vikings in Britain

When the Vikings first landed on the coasts of Britain, they made fast, surprise attacks, and then sailed back to Scandinavia with their plunder. But gradually, some of them decided that they would like to stay in this fertile and peaceful land. They built houses for themselves and became farmers and fishermen. Today, many places in England still have Viking names.

Most of the Vikings who landed in the south and east of England were from Denmark. At that time, England was divided up into a number of small kingdoms. The people who lived in these kingdoms were called Anglo-Saxons. The largest of the Anglo-Saxon kingdoms, in the south-west, was called Wessex. Alfred, the king of Wessex, was a brave man, but he was forced to flee from the Vikings and hide in the marshes.

A battle between Danish Vikings and the Anglo-Saxons.

The Danes in England

More and more of the Danish Vikings poured into England. They overran the south and east, and took complete control of Alfred's kingdom of Wessex. But King Alfred was a clever man. From his hideout in the marshes he began to gather together an Anglo-Saxon army, which was soon strong enough to fight the Danes.

At first, Alfred and his men made quick, daring raids against the Danes. Finally Alfred defeated them in battle, and was able to make an agreement. He would keep his kingdom of Wessex. The Danes would rule the centre and north of England. The part of England governed by the Danish Vikings was called the Danelaw; because Danish, not English law ruled there.

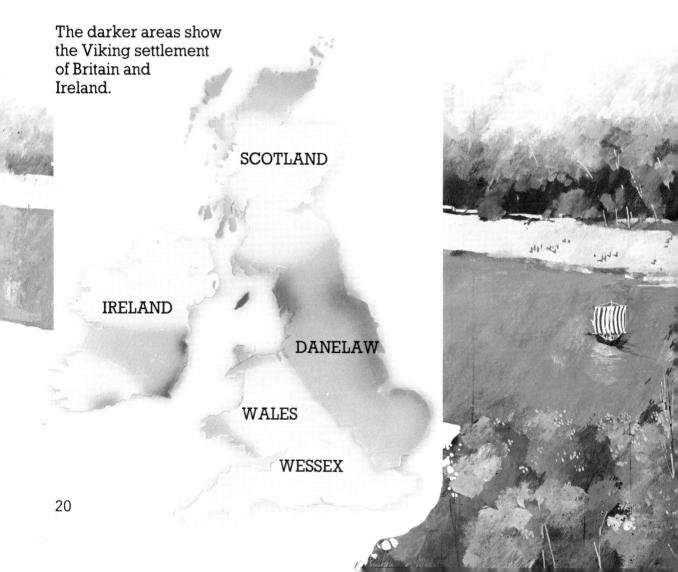

The darker areas show the Viking settlement of Britain and Ireland.

SCOTLAND

IRELAND

DANELAW

WALES

WESSEX

Ethelred and Knut

Long after Alfred's death, a weak king came to the throne of Wessex. He was called Ethelred the Unready. The word "unready" means "badly advised." Ethelred tried to blackmail the Danes to stay out of England by giving them money, called Danegeld. But the Danes, seeing how weak he was, drove him out of his own kingdom. Once again they were in charge of the whole of southern England. Their king, Knut (also spelt Canute), ruled both his English and Danish kingdoms well and wisely. When foolish men told him that even the sea would obey him, Knut showed them that it would not – he sat on the shore and told the waves to go back. Of course, they did not!

A Viking fleet entering England.

21

Sailing westwards

The Vikings sailed westwards from their homelands far across the sea. First they found the island of Iceland. Many Vikings made their homes there. One of them was called Eric the Red – because of his red hair. He sailed further west from Iceland and discovered Greenland. Greenland is very cold with little good land for farming.

Eric the Red's son, Leif Eriksson, decided to sail even further west in search of better land. He and his men braved the cold seas nobody had dared to sail before. At last he reached the coast of North America.

He called the new land Vinland, which means "wine land." At first the Vikings got on well with the Indians who lived there. They gave the Indians beads in exchange for furs. But after three years the Indians turned against the Vikings and drove them away.

The Greenland Vikings hunted whales for food. This was a dangerous business.

Although friendly at first,
the Indians soon drove the
Vikings out of Vinland.

23

Treasures of the East

The Vikings would have heard about the treasures of the East from merchants who travelled to towns like Hedeby. How excited they must have been by the stories of a land filled with silks and spices! The Vikings travelled across Russia, following the rivers down to the Black Sea, and Constantinople (Istanbul), capital city of the fabulous empire of Byzantium. When the rivers were too shallow, the Vikings had to get out of their ships and carry them across the land. Sometimes they took a camel train across the desert to Persia.

The Vikings in Russia

About eleven hundred years ago, three Viking brothers went to Russia. The people who lived there called the Vikings "the Rus." They asked the three brothers to rule over them. The land the brothers ruled came to be called "the land of the Rus." This is where the name "Russia" comes from.

Towards the South

Other Vikings did not stay in Russia. They travelled south to Constantinople – a city of great wealth and splendour. It was ruled by an emperor. The Christian empire of Byzantium traded and fought with other countries round the Mediterranean sea. But the emperor had never seen anything like the wild Vikings, who brought furs in exchange for silks.

The emperor of Byzantium was so impressed with the Vikings, that he asked some of them to stay and act as his bodyguard. They terrified the emperor's enemies.

Kings and lords

Gradually, the small kingdoms of Scandinavia joined together to form three separate countries, Norway, Sweden and Denmark. The king of each surrounded himself with a bodyguard, called the "hird." The most important people after the kings were the lords, called jarls – our word "earl" is almost the same. The kings and the jarls had to be good fighters. The kings often fought each other, as well as the peoples of other countries.

The kings and the jarls owned the land, and they had slaves to work on their farms. The slaves were called thralls. Some of them were men and women captured by the Vikings in far-away countries. The Viking poets, called skalds, did not own land but they were still very important. Their poems were handed down from father to son. This was how the Vikings remembered their history.

A Viking king and his jarls at a feast.

Sometimes the Viking kings found it difficult to keep their lands in order. They built fortresses where soldiers could stay to keep an eye on the countryside.

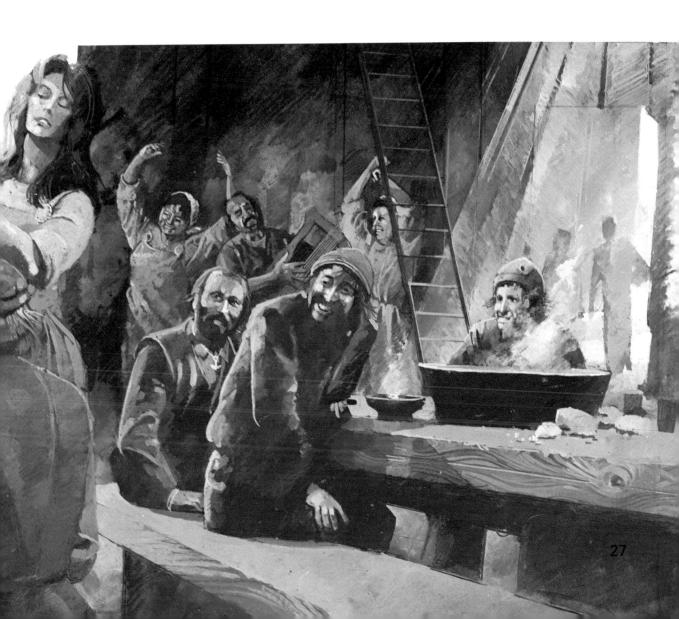

Gods and heroes

The Vikings believed in many different gods. They loved exciting stories about the gods' lives and adventures. The stories were sung by skalds at feasts. The leader of the gods was Odin. He was like the cleverest, and most powerful Viking chief you could ever imagine. Another god was Thor. He made the noise of thunder with his great hammer. Frey was the name of the god who made the crops grow in the earth. He was the special god of farmers. The Viking heaven was called Valhalla.

A hero's death

The Vikings thought that the best way to die was fighting bravely in battle – a man who did this was called a hero. He was buried with his sword and his horse. After death, his spirit would go to Valhalla. Here he would meet many other heroes and they would all feast and drink with the gods.

A Viking burial, and a gravestone carved with runes.

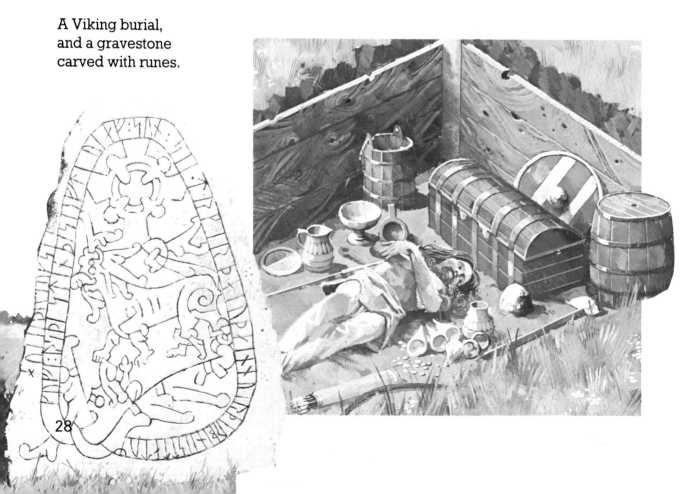

A wooden Viking church.

Viking warriors wore models of the god Thor's hammer to bring them good luck. When they became Christians, they wore the cross instead.

The Viking king, Saint Olaf, shown below, made the Norwegians become Christian. Then they built churches instead of burning them.

29

The last of the Vikings

By the twelfth century, the
Vikings had all become
Christian and lost their
fierce, roving ways. But
these ruins in far-flung
Greenland are a reminder
of the amazing voyages the
Vikings once made.

Glossary

Althing An assembly of people formed by the Vikings when they went to Iceland. It made decisions about the way the new settlement was ruled.

Amber A hard, yellowish, glowing resin. When polished, it is used for ornaments such as beads.

Byzantium A Christian empire based around the city of Constantinople.

Danegeld Large sums of money given to the Danish Vikings by the English, in order to stop their fierce raids.

Danelaw The area of England which was ruled by the Vikings and subject to Danish laws.

Fjord A narrow inlet of the sea between high banks or cliffs.

Jarl A nobleman or chieftain just below the king.

Runes Letters of a special alphabet used by the Vikings for writing, especially on stone. Runic symbols were also believed to have magical powers.

Saga A story about a person from history or legend.

Thrall A servant or slave.

Valhalla The hall where those who have died in battle feast with the god Odin.

Index

PRINTED IN BELGIUM BY

proost
INTERNATIONAL BOOK PRODUCTION